A
Game Theory Approach
to
Mediation

also by Kevin Boileau

Theory

Genuine Reciprocity and Group Authenticity
(First Edition)

Genuine Reciprocity and Group Authenticity:
(The Social Ontology of Sartre & Foucault)

The Algebra of History
(with David A. Boileau)

Essays on Phenomenology and the Self

Manifesto on Solidarity; Ethics for a New World

The Myth of Mediation Neutrality

Coming Soon

Phenomenology
& Mediation

Critical Existential
Psycho-Analysis

Workbook for Psychoanalysis
& Mediation

Vivantonomy
A Trans-Humanist
Phenomenology of the Self

Literary

The Patient

The Blue Pearl

Abject Poverty

99 Deceptions

The Separation

The Return

The Outlaw Series Vol. 1

Make Me Stay

Sexxual Lies

A Turtle's Murder

Coming Soon

Northside

The Bishop... A Fisherman

3 Rivers

Sweet Monogamy

BCS

BCS Dispute Resolution is dedicated to producing useful and informative texts in mediation, negotiation, and dispute resolution design. Based on research in phenomenology, psychoanalysis, critical theory, and game theory mathematics, the books that we produce present innovative theory and practice to teachers, scholars, and professionals in the fields of dispute resolution, including mediators, lawyers, negotiators, psychologists, collaborative facilitators, life coaches, and specialized family lenders/Realtors.

For more information:
solutionsbcs@gmail.com
www.boileaucs.com
www.bcsmediationtraining.com

EPIS Press
31 Fort Missoula Road, Suite 4
Missoula, MT 59804 USA
epispublishing1@gmail.com

Printed in the United States of America
First Edition February 2015

Library of Congress Cataloging-in-Publication Data
1. Game Theory 2. Mediation 3. Prisoners Dilemma
4. Mediation training   I Title

Cover Design: Peggy Sands
Interior Book Design: Tia Hopkins
Author Photo: NTG
Author Seal: Adrian Balasa

ISBN 978-0-9899301-4-7

A
Game Theory Approach
to
Mediation

Overcoming the Prisoner's Dilemma

A Short Introduction

VOLUME 2

in the Mediation Book Series

Dr. Kevin Boileau
Ph.D., J.D., LL.M.

Contents

Foreword

This book is the second in a series of books for professional mediators and for parties involved in conflict who think they need mediation. I consider this book to be very introductory and straightforward. Moreover, I consider it to be helpful for any mediation practitioner. The reason is simple: mathematics does not lie. Instead it explains and clarifies one's conflict situation. It is a corrective methodology and, as such, can bring rationality, fairness, and equanimity into a conflict resolution process. This introductory volume does not include any mathematics other than a few simple diagrams, and I believe that this simplicity is its introductory strength. I leave for the next volume more complicated renderings and analysis.

I also leave for another day an account of resolution processes such as duels, trials, and other aggressive, adversary methods. In contrast, this book assumes a basic situation whose elements include the following: a couple seeking a divorce with capabilities of rationality even though they are stressed and experience strong emotions; the involvement of a professional mediator; a legal divorce process in a court; the parties' willingness to try to work things out cooperatively; and a way to discuss a divorce resolution that is understandable by both parties as well as a mediator.

I am both a lawyer and psychoanalyst, and am therefore sensitive to both the legal issues and the psychological issues in a divorce case as well as in any conflict in general. I actively mediate a number of conflicts, especially those in divorce and family law. I direct research institutes in psychoanalysis and in dispute resolution, and spend a good deal of time writing about these issues. As a scientist, I approach this book with an exploratory attitude and strong belief that its contents will be quite helpful to the reader, especially if he or she is involved in mediation or is a party to a mediation case.

BCS Dispute Resolution Research Institute has a clear mission of understanding conflict and its resolution with insightful analysis and practical applications. It is involved in a number of research programs and projects, big and small. Several of these have found their way into professional mediation trainings across North America, and several are being developed. The Institute is also the host of an academic and professional journal concerning game theory and conflict, and the institutional support for the book series of which this volume is a part.

I am writing this book as a part of a series whose mission is to develop the practice of mediation into a much more refined, efficient, and fair dispute resolution process. In a sense, at the Institute we are engaged in dispute resolution design, for mediation is a specific form of conflict resolution that is different from other types such as duel and trial. It has its own precepts and protocols, and it is our aim to dialogue with others about them and to improve the overall resolution situation. In this book here we focus solely on the divorce situation although in future work we will address business negotiation, organizational conflict, workplace conflict, and more.

Our plan is to write at least one short book that explains each of our trainings. This is a tall order, to be sure, but each subject area is important to the overall mediation environment, interesting and valuable in its own right, and therefore informs our future intent. Our first book was on the application of psychoanalysis to mediation, especially the idea of the unconscious, which is a radically different philosophy of mind than what most professionals are used to; however, we think it applicable and valuable, and another piece of the overall puzzle of conflict and its resolution. This topic here — game theory — is the subject of one of our research projects at the Institute and has a clear integration with psychoanalysis as part of a methodology that will deepen our understanding of mediation and elevate the standards of practice.

Game theory is a theory about decision-making in conditions of uncertainty. It involves imperfect information, informal and formal rules, strategies and tactics, potential payoffs to the players. Usually, interests of the participants are not completely co-extensive, and to this extent, game theory helps us explain the decision-making environment, the way we communicate our interests and preferences, and the way we ultimately negotiate settlement or agreement. In mediation, there is an endpoint, for the parties ultimately make written agreements to which they affix their signatures. In our research and in our practice, we have an overarching normative goal of attempting to optimize sustainable solution sets. This is the very heart of mediation as theory and practice. We focus on 2-person games such as divorce, although our research has, of course, applicability to n-person games, such as the ones we see in organizational conflict management.

Finally, while our work is new, it is built on the shoulders of a number of theorists and practitioners who have come before us. As in any scientific inquiry, we do not know where our work will lead us. However, it is our strong desire to illuminate situation of interpersonal difference and conflict and, in this case here, in the context of divorce. My hope is that by the time the reader finishes this text, he or she will have some new ideas about the value of game theory for the practice and understanding of mediation.

Finally, this volume is very introductory. It does not explore intermediate or advanced levels of game theory. It does not delineate any of the mathematical symbolization that we will address in future volumes. It does, however, provide the reader—a mediation practitioner—with a starting point.

Kevin Boileau, PhD, JD/LLM
Writing in Missoula, Montana
United States
May 2014

Chapter 1

Introduction to Divorce Mediation Situation

The divorce situation is a major life transition, which can result in positive growth and transformation but which can also bring stress, emotional deregulation, and a series of largely irrational behaviors that are often destructive. As such, there is a dialectical process between the cooperative and the adversarial, the rational and the emotional. This process always creates a dynamic between the parties and the mediator, which is one of the exciting and interesting elements of this sort of work. One day a divorcing spouse can be level headed, rational, and productive in her communication. On other days, however, the same person can be adversarial, emotionally deregulated, and unproductive. Let me explain.

Everyone has a fight or flight response attached to his more primitive, limbic brain stem. In divorce there is often much to be worried about, including children, finances, living space, friends, acquaintances, work, personal identity, assets, and vacation homes. Everything is in flux and there is a great deal of uncertainty about the way things will be in the future. In cases where a spouse is being left unilaterally, there are prominent self-esteem issues as well. More often than not, new relationships are already part of the dynamic, so there are emotional vulnerabilities and hurt feelings that emerge. As such, it is easy for two parties to either become outwardly aggressive or passive, along with intermittent periods of calm rationality. Part of the mediator's job is to contain these oscillations in a productive and cooperative way, facilitating the movement from competition to cooperation whenever possible. This restores the autonomy of each party in such a way that each can make a fully informed decision about important elements of the marital dissolution.

Divorce is a death of sorts, of dreams, hopes, unmet needs, lost hopes, unresolved psychological issues, and emergent regressions of historical traumas. This triggers stress along with reconsideration of whom one is. The self-concept is put into question as divorcing parties disentangle a complex relationship with a number of individual attachments, leaving them in a state of ontological rupture. This has both positive and negative

1

elements: the positive involves a new sense of freedom, and often individuals in this transition explore dreams and desires that they had put on hold; however, there is also a negative dimension because of fear and anxiety over being able to move forward in life. Thus, all elements of a grieving process are present, but it is complicated because even though the marriage is dying the other spouse is still alive, becoming someone new and different (in the eyes of each of the marriage partners).

What is often complicated is that each spouse is in a different stage of the grieving process. Usually one spouse is the initiator of the divorce and the other spouse is the follower. Thus, the initiating spouse is already moving forward with a new life, which can include a new romantic interest, a separate living space, separate bank account, and so forth. In this case, the following spouse is often in a complicated state of anger, denial, and confusion, which can make it difficult to negotiate important goods in a divorce. In the rare instance in which both spouses are at similar stages of grieving, there is still the oscillation between adversarial self-protection and cooperative regard for the other. It is a delicate process, and is profoundly affected by the quality and skill of the mediator handling the case.

To make matters more stressful, it is usually the case that even highly reflective individuals either lack understanding of the divorce process or have false information they have received from others. These false beliefs can escalate anxieties to substantial proportions and unfortunately steer the process—even with an experienced professional—into an adversarial dynamic, even though the parties do not recognize it as such, or cannot articulate it discursively, which is the beginning of rational and productive resolution. Thus, part of the mediation process involves a very important education phase about the facts of the matter as well as typical false beliefs that derail cooperative processes.

Once the parties are significantly aware of how the family courts work, the nature of divorce mediation, and typical communication dynamics that lead to "non-zero-sum" outcomes, they each can begin to think about needs and preferences in a way that can be fairly negotiated with his or her spouse. This involves the splitting of bank accounts, assets, time with children, timing of transfers and changes, changes in social relationships, extended family relationships, and any other value item. Some people focus entirely on numbers; others focus on transitions in important relationships. These foci are expressions of subjective values, and become important foundations of mediation agreements. In short, they are the items that conflict parties in this situation fight about and later come to mutually beneficial agreements.

Let us imagine what a cooperative process consists of behaviorally and dynamically, and then let us compare that to an adversarial process. We will start with common sense views and intuitions and then as we progress through our book we will add game theory concepts to our basic ideas. This will help us refine our understanding of the divorce situation as well as integrate our general understandings of cooperation and conflict with an analytical view that supplements our intuitions. Let us now discuss some of the specific dimensions of the conflict situation in divorce from a practical point of view.

In our practice and in our research we see that most individuals want to protect their rights, which usually involves property, money, and children. The idea of cooperation seems to be a dimension that is layered on top of a rights-based approach for many individuals. Coupled with an inadequate understanding of the law and the process, this easily leads highly cooperative people toward conflict. This occurs because rights are individual, and frequently there are incompatible needs and preferences with regard to some important aspect of the external goods for which the parties compete. On the other hand, some individuals are secure enough in their own rights, abilities, or their spouse's sense toward fairness that their starting point just is cooperation and mutuality. These cases are more rare than the first, and we can easily imagine that if a couple has an adequate mutual dynamic they might not be interested in divorce in the first instance. Let's take the most important goods in order, discussing both the cooperative aspects as well as the adversarial ones.

Issues concerning marital houses and secondary properties can be complex and problematic because of their practical aspects. Separating out one financial system into two can require new loan qualifications, ample cash, and often the cooperation of both parties. There are timing issues as well that require a tolerance for patience and a step by step plan that will detach the parties from each other in their property ownership. If they are cooperative this can usually happen especially because there is a statutory wait period within which title transfers, refinancing, and cash payouts can occur. Nevertheless, because of the stress involved even parties with substantial equanimity can fall prey to anxiety, distrust, and destructive self-protection. This changes the communication from a cooperative dynamic to an adversarial one, and if the mediation process does not reverse this course, some cases can end up in litigation.

Issues concerning cash accounts and savings accounts are normally minimal because these are easy to split and are helpful in facilitating other property transfers. When these accounts are retirement accounts there are splitting fees, but this process is straightforward and time sensitive. Where this part of the equation can turn destructive is in cases in which one of the parties either has an irrational attachment to more than half of the cash or in which they make a strong claim to have contributed more than fifty percent some time in the past. It is important to highlight the point that what seems fair and just to an outside perspective might not be to the parties because of internal historical facts that might be hard to discern.

Conflicts concerning children are particularly rife with complexity because of inherent bonds between parents and children, and their emotional dimension. Fathers fear losing their children; mothers are usually steadfast in protecting their best interest, sometimes irrationally so. The point is that irrational factors can easily emerge in parenting plan negotiations and interrupt what could be a straightforward process. Because there are usually a number of details involved in agreeing to childcare and individual parenting responsibilities, there are several triggers for contention and numerous possibilities for conflict. Moreover, it is often the case that divorcing couples sometimes lack the strong sympathy and empathy that used to be present in each for the other. In these cases—and I don't mean to imply that financial issues are not extant too—the ability to be rational is useful and efficient. Thus, when the situation becomes more businesslike and less replete with feelings, the ability to utilize a fair and rational analytic process is crucial.

Even when couples are able to peacefully and cooperatively resolve difference concerning money, property, and children, there are numerous other issues that can trigger strong emotions, including changing social relations with neighbors, other family members, friends, co-workers, and acquaintances. Old wounds emerge. Personal issues come to the fore. In these dimensions, conflict may seem to be between the spouses but sometimes this is not the case; sometimes the conflict is internal. However, it is easy to imagine the difficulty in being empathetic and cooperative in these areas because of one's own personal struggles. This may require careful interim agreements regarding these issues that protect the continued stability of the process. New sexual and romantic partners further complicate cooperative possibilities, as do substance abuse issues, personality disorders, and hidden issues that start to surface.

The basic tension is between higher-level moral thinking/empathy (which is a transformative approach) and lower level, limbic brain stem feeling/thinking (which is defensive and often adversarial). This is the opportunity for a competent mediator to facilitate rationality and efficiency, and a co-parenting relationship if there are children involved. Even if the parties no longer have soft feelings for each other, they still have a choice between cooperation and competition at every juncture in the mediation and dissolution process. At this point in our discussion it will be helpful to describe the Prisoner's Dilemma, which is a game that illustrates the tension between cooperation and competition in terms of adhering to or defecting from agreements. It is to this game that we now turn, before moving to the next chapter, which is an introduction to the philosophy and reasoning underneath a game theory approach to mediation.

In the Prisoner's Dilemma, there are 2 thieves who make an agreement to never provide evidence against the other in case they get caught. One day they do get caught, are separated into two interrogation rooms, and each has to decide whether to keep their agreement—or defect. There are 4 outcomes: One, each keeps the agreement and they are sentenced to three months in jail. Two, they both defect and receive six years in prison. Three [and four], one defects and the other maintains the agreement. In this case the defector receives no time in jail or prison; the other received nine years. Thus, the outcomes are: 0 time, 3 months, 6 years, and 9 years.

The decision-making environment is primarily one of uncertainty because neither party knows what the other will choose. Let's look at it from Thief A's perspective: If Thief B keeps the agreement, it is better for A to defect, for this moves his outcome from 3 months to 0. If, however, B defects, then it is better for A to defect, for this moves his outcome from 9 years to 6 years.

The divorce situation is analogous the Prisoner's Dilemma because there are two parties who have the option to cooperate or compete in conditions of uncertainty. They don't know what each other will do, and although they may feel cooperative with each other, they will each have the inherent desire for self-protection and survival. Thus, there is a dialectical tension in each divorcing party to compete and to cooperate. Nevertheless, game theory mathematics implies that the best choice is always to defect from the agreement. Of course, this doesn't address internal goods such as keeping agreements, being cooperative, correcting moral behavior, and the like. Typical game theory analysis does not address these internal and subjective goods because they have been though un-measurable. In a sense this is correct, and especially in terms of the language and focus of the justice system. To be clear, divorce courts decide issues such as bank accounts, property, and children, and not internal goods such as honesty, subjective apprehensions of moral behavior, and sympathy. Thus, at one level, in a solid game theory analysis, we should only look at external goods and subjective preference about them. We will leave to another day, perhaps a deeper analysis that includes the psychological [and often unconscious internal goods] that are not decided in courts. It is important, though, for the reader to carefully reflect on the situation exemplified by the Prisoner's Dilemma, and the inherent dilemma between cooperation and competition in the divorce scenario.

Finally, it is important to note that the mediation process is a communication situation. It involves listening to one another and listening by a mediator. It will inform he mediator about the values, worldviews, and possibilities for each party. This will set the factual foundation for a game theory mathematical analysis by a mediator; this in turn will help the mediator understand the specific tension between cooperation and competition in a particular case between specific and unique individuals.

We will see in the chapters that follow how this sort of understanding can help a qualified mediator to transform an anxiety-ridden divorce process into a full cooperative, highly efficient and fair mediation—with a long-term, sustainable outcome.

Chapter 2

A Game Theory Approach Improves Rational Thinking

In order to appreciate the benefits of incorporating game theory into a divorce mediation process, we must first understand the decision-making landscape without it. As such, I need to make a few comments in that direction. In general, mediation is becoming more professionalized than ever before. Nevertheless, there is somewhat of a lack of standardization in the field, and a number of practitioners who have significantly different approaches and orientations in their work.

The mediation field is replete with practitioners who have some level of training in the following areas: law, psychology and behavior, communication, high conflict personalities, containment of strong emotions, writing an agreement, parenting, and topics relating to mortgage, real estate, and banking. There is no substitute for experience, and a varied history with a number of different types of scenarios. For those practitioners who are paralegals, lawyers, or who are associated with a law practice, there is an acquaintance with court forms and processes as they integrated with the mediation itself.

Many mediators are excellent communicators, some with business backgrounds, and others with counseling in their histories, which brings insight and empathy oriented sensitivities into their practices. Still others, who have some level of experience and training in all the aforementioned areas, also have some education in negotiation theory and practice. There are now national programs that are growing in sophistication and rigor, both at the continuing education level and at the formal, university level. In many instances, professional approach cases with some combination of this knowledge, experience, and perspective. I think it is often the case that there is a focus on empathy and sympathy, utilizing each party's sense of mutuality as a motive for cooperative resolution. This, in combination with careful marshaling of the facts, including mathematic figures, tends toward optimization of very resources and goods that the parties are splitting.

However, all this practical wisdom, including careful banking and accounting calculations, lacks inquiry into unconscious forces and dynamics (which I lay out in my The Myth of Mediation Neutrality). It also lacks a concession to the mathematics of game theory, which can help us understand—in a purely objective way—the possibilities for decision-making when the other party's choices are uncertain. Knowledge in this area can be immensely valuable for a conflict resolution professional, and quite helpful to the parties. This contains at least two components: First, it offers a rational, objective, and clear way for any and all human beings to understand the decision-making situation. Second, taking into account a game theory perspective helps us formulate objective and fair standards, which can create and maintain equilibrium in the a mediation process.

Keep in mind that marital dissolution is a complex decision-making environment that involves uncertainties, strong emotions, and anxiety about one's future as marriage is separated. Game theory mathematics just is a way of looking at decision-making, in any context, although we are focusing on divorce. What makes this situation susceptible to a game theory analysis is that involves the choices of the other spouse as well as chance. That is, along with the uncertainties of one's spouse's choices, there is also the fact that the environment itself changes through time: We have seen people lose jobs, gain promotions, die, suffer catastrophic loss, moving out of state, and the like during the statutory wait period. This is what I mean by a changing environment. Usually, however, these changes are smaller in scope, but even so we cannot predict out spouse's actions in this changing environment. It is these unpredictable actions that game theory addresses, by looking at the definable choices of each spouse, constructing a decision-matrix, and then computing outcomes and their values.

Let us drill down into a game theory worldview. By translating an often confusing, emotional, and in some cases, financially complex into this mathematical construct, we can view the spouses as players of a [hopefully rational] game, each with individual strategies, and both will eventual payoffs. We can understand strategic propensities through personality indices and psychoanalytic taxonomies because they give us statistical insight into likely moves in a divorce game. However, this research is still nascent [though helpful] and (something I broach in my recently published The Myth of Mediation Neutrality), which means at this point, a game theoretical analysis of a divorce can greatly facilitate a rational mediation process. I also want to highlight that this "game" is one of imperfect and changing information; this is partially why these situations lead to anxiety and stress, and definitely one of the main reasons why competent mediation is so helpful.

A psychoanalytic view replaces the idea that we can ever be fully autonomous agents with the view that much of what motivates us is unconscious. It is complicated theoretically, and complicated in its application. However, it is my belief that eventually we will be able to add unconscious factors to a more complete [and more accurate] game theory analysis. Without the psychoanalytic factors, we can still entertain a very accurate analysis that is based on a model of rational choice theory, including the assumption that the parties will make the best choices possible that will eventually lead to mutual optimization of resources. A game theory analysis can be done in every divorce case, and graphs can be constructed that are useful teaching aids for the facilitation of a successful mediation.

What I like about a game theory approach is that it is supplemental to all the other processes that I have mentioned before. It does not replace them, but instead enhances their usefulness, in my experience. Just by looking at options, especially on paper, the parties assuage themselves. This occurs because people like choice, and they enjoy the freedom to make those choices. A game theory matrix illustrates this. Yet, it goes further because it delineates these choices and their outcomes with great precision. This helps to form a detailed, comprehensive view of the choices and their outcomes. We can do this because each case is a closed system of sorts even though the situation may evolve and transform. It is a closed system because the major components of what will be mediated are always identifiable and finite amounts and values. Additional, smaller items are easily negotiated once the major issues are settled, in my experience. The main point, however, stands because the components of a closed system can be compared, and valued, and this creates opportunities for optimized calculations. Moreover, most individuals will recognize that the mathematics is true independent of their opinions and subjective judgments about value. This sets an independent standard—a methodology—that both parties recognize is fair. This, in turn, creates stability and equanimity in the process; it also allows for independent, efficient, third party review of this fair process.

This neutral and objectively fair methodology has many advantages. In addition to calming the parties and allowing for easy independent review, game theory analysis can aid mediators in talking with clients, each of the parties discussing the various components of their agreement with each other, and securing the framework for a finalized written agreement. This is not to say that humans are completely rational but this methodology does provide us with a way to correct our irrational, indignant, and unfair impulses. That is to say that it creates a framework for dialogue and review. This serves the overall mediation goal of sustainability as well as setting an expectation for any future behaviors between soon-to-be ex-spouses, such as co-parenting arrangements. Let us now proceed to the next chapter, in which I use a hypothetical case to illustrate—in an introductory way—some of the dynamics of a divorce mediation case that includes the dimension of game theory mathematics.

Chapter 3

Paradigm Case
That Illustrates Game Theory

This is the right place in our exploration to present a hypothetical case, and amongst other items, to discuss the game theory dimension in an introductory way. In this case, which we will call the "Smith-Jones" case, there is a couple in their late-thirties, including Smith the husband and Jones the wife. They met abroad at a work function, later got married, and then moved to the United States with good jobs in the technology industry. Within a few years, the wife, Jones, became pregnant, and the couple decided that she would quite her job and that Smith, the husband, would become the sole breadwinner of the young family. Thus, the family went forward without the wife's $200,000 annual salary, even though the husband received a promotion and a pay raise to $300,000 per year.

For a few years, the marriage continued unabated, along with a new child who was growing in a healthy and happy way. Unfortunately, the husband traveled out of the country regularly for his job, and eventually the marriage suffered. The husband, Smith, continued excelling in his work, and received substantial bonuses for the next few years, although they were unpredictable in amount. After one of the out of country trips, the couple had a significant conflict and decided to get a divorce. Under their plan, they would cooperate with each other, co-parent their child, and move to a cheaper state, into separate homes. After much deliberation, they decided to hire a mediator to get them through the whole dissolution.

They had the following assets: a $1.5m home with a $600,000 mortgage; $250,000 in savings; $65,000 in checking; $600,000 retirement account for Smith ($100,000 started prior to the marriage); $75,000 retirement account for Jones; approximately $55,000 worth of furniture and household items; personal effects worth an unknown amount; and art/jewelry worth $30,000 – 100,000, depending upon whether Smith or Jones is estimating. They do seem fair and reasonable, however, and from the outside it looks like this case can be negotiated.

Because they'd both heard positive things about mediation, and because it was so much cheaper than litigation, they entered mediation with optimism and open-minded attitudes. They paid the retainer, signed the letter of engagement, and agreed to a series of individual and joint meetings designed to quickly and efficiently get them to a written mediation agreement and a filing of the court documents. These meetings began and all seemed to go well for a few weeks. Then it became apparent that the husband was trying to dominate the process. In contrast, the wife seemed to want to get through the mediation as quickly as possible. Her agreements seemed unreflective as long as she had access to the family credit cards and her life continued as usual. Both parties seemed eager to move on with their lives. In a couple of weeks they took trips out of state to a new city to where they were both moving because the cost of living was cheaper. The plan was to find separate places to live. Then they returned to their marital home to continue with the mediation process.

The mediators on the case did the statutory calculations internally to see what a family court would order for child support and for spousal support. Through continued discussion with both spouses, it became clear that neither one cared about the statutory calculation, opting instead for they both agreed would be fair and necessary for each and for both, keeping in mind the needs of their one child, a daughter. The husband started complaining that their initial agreement paid her too much, and that the child support should be decreased as well. Evidently, he was afraid that the move would negatively affect his value to his company. It was also true that almost one-half of his income for the past was due to a complex bonus system about which he was fretful that he would not receive his usual amount. In contrast, his wife wanted to stick more or less to what they had initially agreed on, clearly desiring to move on quickly. One point of contention was that she did not work and had little motivation to get a job anytime soon because of the ample support her husband provided. Although she did mention getting a job in a couple of years it was no concern to her presently, which made her husband nervous. There were other issues as well, concerning childcare, holidays, and travel, but we can address those later. For now, let's approach this situation from a game theory perspective.

Recall that game theory assumes that the parties are rational, which we know is not completely true; however, this provides us with an analytical starting point for discussion. The starting point is that they were in an uncertain strategic situation in which they had both made an agreement to cooperate with each other. Whether they were in good faith with this agreement was yet to be seen. So, let's start with the major components of the [game] transaction, which included the property, money, the husband's income, and the proposed parenting plan for the child. The basic elements are as follows: The parents would split custody even though the mother, Jones, would take on most of the duties in reality; this would occur because the father, Smith, would continue traveling extensively. They originally proposed an income average of a) his highest income with bonus and b) his lowest, base income without bonus. This average was $225,000 to which they both agreed even though the mediators sensed apprehension in Smith, the husband-father. This left $575,000 in shared retirement, $315,000 in cash (before they would have to pay $50,000 in bills), $900,000 equity in the house, and $120,000 average value in shared household and personal effects. It was also true that because the wife didn't work she wouldn't be able to qualify for a loan on a new house. They both agreed to immediately sell their house.

The reader may think that these two spouses would quibble about the split each would get from the assets and cash accounts, but it was here that they found easy agreement. Their conflict centered in the amounts offered for child and spousal support, as well as time with their daughter. Let's take these in reverse order: Smith, the father, wanted the court documents to reflect equal parenting time even though it was clear that his would be more 25% at most because of his travel. This inaccuracy bothered Jones, his wife. More importantly, they started to disagree about Smith's stated income because this could affect child and spousal support. For the past few years he'd made a base salary and a bonus that matched the base, but he was worried that he might be paying future support based on bonuses he might never receive. Thus, a problem emerged: She wanted him to claim $300,000 annual income and he wanted to claim $150,000—along with comments that he'd "be generous with them if he received his bonuses." Jones, the wife, did not feel comfortable with that. Let us hold our thoughts about the facts of the case, and turn to the topic of preferences, which can be articulated through utility theory. Then we will return to a descriptive account of the games these parties seemed to be playing.

Utility theory suggests that each party ranks their preferences relative to each other, and that these preferences may shift through time as the situation itself changes. Some of these preferences are conscious and others perhaps somewhat unconscious, but to the extent we are aware we enter into quantifications of our preferences in the context of a game, i.e. a mediation process, relative to the other party's own preferences. There are some problems with trying to construct a utility function for spouse's decisions in a mediated divorce. First, people change their preferences through time, which incidentally, can derail an already-successful mediation. Second, people choose based on inconsistent, irregular, and irrelevant factors and any important to fit them into a rational model is illusory. Even so, in my experience, and in the case at hand, I have discovered that people do make comparisons in preferences; they rank these preferences; they do gamble if the odds are good enough; and in the end we can make some helpful observations about these choices. How we can account for them mathematically is more problematic because of unconscious and irrational factors. Let's see if we can make any sense out of the instant couple's individual choices as a way to deepen our game theory approach. Remember, my goal is to move us into an introductory game theory way of thinking.

The husband in our case has a few preferences: he wants access to his child; he wants to spend the minimum amount of money possible on the divorce and on spousal support while appearing to meet his obligations; on this note, he wanted a fair split of their money and assets; he didn't actually want the divorce but accepts his wife's choice and therefore wants to move forward quickly; he also wants his life to be convenient in the future. In parallel fashion, his wife also wanted to move forward as quickly as possible; her priority was the happiness of their child; she spent money generously but realized that protecting monies for her child was essential; she wanted her husband to be fair with support but trusted him to do so. She was also clear that she wanted to move in with her new single life. Both were significantly rational and cooperative in my judgment, the only two major sources of anxiety revolving around the father's access to his child and his desire not to overspend his (and their) budget.

In short, I chose to discuss this case because it was relatively straightforward and the parties are relatively rational and cooperative. By understanding a simple case, we can clarify how preferences structuralize a type of game, and how it is situated in the dialectic between cooperation and competition, whether it is played as a non-zero-sum game or as a zero-sum game. A full analysis would require us to assign numbers to their preferences, assign utilities, thereby constructing a matrix that reveals comparative preferences. Let's leave that task for now and explore in a preliminary and descriptive way the games they are playing. Smith, the husband, tries to dominate the dynamic, even in mediation, and is cooperative but only when he gets his way. When he does not get his way he becomes argumentative and aggressive. He plays a competitive game within the limits of what appears cooperative. His wife, in contrast, is easily cooperative, and will do anything, accede to anything, and compromise anything, for that goal. In the financial dimension, she compromised at every turn in the road in order to accelerate the process. She appeared to fully cooperate as long as the transaction was within the bounds of fairness.

While it may be true that they were playing several games, they were also playing the Prisoner's Dilemma game, which I mentioned earlier in this text. For purposes of learning, at this point let's only discuss the Prisoner's Dilemma. In future sections, we will add discussion about other games and considerations. Recall that in the Prisoner's Dilemma Game ("PDG"), each party can adhere to their agreement to cooperate through a mediated divorce or each could defect in various ways and with differing levels of openness about the defection. We can see that defining cooperation can be complex and even difficult because the scenario is dynamic and includes a number of factors with a range of behavioral responses. In fact, sometimes it can be difficult to discern how much a party is actually adhering to an agreement to cooperate and how much a party is defecting. In the PDG, there are 4 outcomes that can be roughly translated to a divorce mediation scenario. Let me try to articulate the basic framework. O time, 3months, 6 years, and 9 years translates as follows: A divorce party, even one who is mediation, always oscillates between protecting himself and cooperating with the other in a way that creates vulnerability. In terms of the game, there are also four basic outcomes, which I can now discuss.

A good but not best result is parallel to thieves both receiving 3 months in jail. In a divorce case it means that both parties work together, perhaps give up some things they thought they preferred, perhaps changing their minds about what they thought they wanted. This type of result creates a sustainable future transformed relationship, for example, if the parties are co-parents; in the event that there is no future relationship contemplated, it creates emotional closure, and thus allows both parties to move forward with their personal lives. In contrast, the third best result is tantamount to both thieves giving evidence against each other and each receiving 6 years in prison. In this case, both divorcing parties stop cooperating with each other, thereby defecting and creating an adversarial dynamic. This costs more money, increases stress, decreases sustainability, and takes much more time and duration. This is a case that moves from mediation to litigation.

The last two results occur when one party defects and the other adheres. In this case, the defector is not really honest about a cooperative mediation or changes his or her mind about cooperation without explicitly saying so to the other. In these circumstances, if drawn out to its natural conclusion, the defector would end up with what seems the best result: more money, more time with the children, or other external goods. However, under this situation it is questionable whether what is gained here is worth what is lost. Even so, without analyzing whether a maximum gain of external goods is really the best result for a party, the one who adheres to the agreement loses much of these precious goods even though he or she may gain in the internal goods involving morality, emotional resolution, and the like. Nevertheless, these cases don't often go to their natural conclusion. Instead, the one adhering quickly realizes the defection and usually follows suit. This ends up in the third best result—and more often than not, litigation. In this case there are two results because who is the defector can switch. In either case, however, these situations end up in adversarial dynamics and a joint loss of goods.

An important constellation of points to note is that parties to a divorce are often compromised in their ability to carefully reason given the amount of stress, normal sadness/anger, and uncertainty that is frequently a part of this process. Most divorcing spouses do not naturally do a game theory analysis and even for the ones who do, the clarity of the matrix might not persuade. However, if a good mediator can help the parties calm themselves by providing a safe container for the process, parties can be led to their most rational selves thereby maximizing their natural autonomy. There is more to a deep game theory analysis but this requires that we elucidate additional concepts, which we are now ready to address in the next chapter.

Diagram #1

		Thief 1	
		Stays Quiet	Rats
Thief 2	Stays Quiet	3 months, 3 months	9 years, 0
	Rats	0, 9 yrs	6 years, 6 years

Classical Prisoner's Dilemma

Diagram #2

		Husband	
		Cooperates	**Competes**
Wife	**Cooperates**	decreases fees, duration, stress; makes co-parenting positive	drives process toward litigation
	Competes	drives process toward litigation	greatly increases fees, frustration, duration, stress; makes co-parenting difficult

Prisoner's Dilemma Applied to Divorce

Chapter 4

Useful Game Theory Concepts for Divorce Mediation

In this chapter, I will introduce some new concepts that help us deepen our understanding of how game theory can be useful in a divorce mediation process. By introducing game theory concepts we can refine and clarify our understanding of the case example above and all the games people regularly play in divorce processes. Let's be clear: divorce can be interpreted as a game. In this dissolution game, each party assesses the extent to which her goals converge with or diverge from the goals of the other spouse. Then he or she must decide whether to cooperate or compete with these goals. This decision determines whether the game is zero-sum or non-zero-sum, being a combination of both mutual and conflicting interests. Calling divorce mediation a game might seem odd, but it thereby allows us a language that we can use for analysis. Within the game there are rules, imperfect and changing information, changing perspectives and preferences, constant uncertainties, and assessments, and perhaps most importantly, an irrational element that is comprised of anxiety, fear, and a constellation of other emotions. Each person will always choose a strategy is a plan of action that he believes will lead to the satisfaction of his or her preferences.

Let me describe the notion of a two-person, zero-sum game. This is how we identify an adversarial, competitive approach that is typical of litigation. It is often an adversarial dynamic because the parties have radically divergent interests. An example of this occurs when each spouse in a divorce wants more time with their children than they want their spouse to have. In this tug-of-war situation each party will negotiate aggressively to maximize his or her time with the children. If neither party can gain by changing his strategy unilaterally then they are in equilibrium. The technical components of equilibrium include the maximin and minimax principles. If they equal each other then the payoff to each and to both is in equilibrium. In this case, each party tries to maximize his minimum (the maximin) and each party tries to minimize the other party's maximum (the minimax).

More specifically, if both parties to the game act reasonably, they will each try to play to the average amount they can expect to win from the other. Usually (but not always) parties try to maximize their time with their children, post-divorce; the paying spouse tries to minimize spousal support and the receiving spouse tries to maximize spousal support; and to a lesser extent each tries to get a bit more than half of the community assets. Although there is lingering psychological tension for the parties, these solutions that are in equilibrium are usually sustainable and stable because over time the parties realize they are fair to both. Dominated strategies, which some aggressive divorcing spouses tend toward, are almost always rejected by the other spouse, and therefore rarely end up in equilibrium (although when this truth becomes known they either lead to it or permanently derail the mediation. The complication is that the parties' interests are not usually completely divergent; they are frequently overlapping. This truth, however, can make the analysis more complex, for then the mediator needs to determine where they are convergent and where they are divergent, given their psychological styles.

In contrast, there is the non-zero-sum game that represents the other end of the continuum in divorce mediation. This is the cooperative end of the pole, which competes with the competitive and protective tendencies in divorcing parties. Recall that in a zero-sum game, one party's gain is the other party's loss. Nevertheless, the zero-sum game is only an ideal, and is rarely the case in divorce mediation. This occurs for a number of reasons, including genuine care and mutuality between divorcing couples, an ongoing co-parenting or similar relationship, or a rational realization that cooperative games are superior to competitive ones in this type of scenario. I must also highlight the fact that in divorce, the games are both cooperative and competitive. There is an oscillation, sometimes daily, between zero-sum and non zero-sum approaches, which is understandable given the inherently stressful circumstance of divorce and the fact that the interests of the parties naturally diverge — more or less.

Nonetheless, even though the party's interests may actually diverge, more often than not, their interests are co-extensive, especially if there is a continuing relationship. It is also common for divorcing parties to perceive that their interests to be antagonistic when actually they are convergent. In rare cases, the parties' interests are almost completely similar. Given that in the majority of cases, there is a divergence of interests, the goal of mediation is to help the divorcing spouses become aware of this tension between cooperation and competition. By using the language of game theory, mediators can go a long way to facilitate this understanding. This can help overcome emotional impediments to a non-zero-sum approach. What I mean here is that sometimes, the parties' own angers and resentments can get in the way of moving toward a cooperative dynamic. In that case, communication is stultified, in some cases, sporadic or non-existent, and not designed to develop mutual-gain sub-agreements as part of an overall cooperative strategy.

In the sort of situation we contemplate, in which divorcing parties choose mediation, what normally and usually happens is that there is a great deal of agreement on most issues — up to a point. These individuals usually choose mediation because something about the cooperative process is intuitively appealing. In these cases, some of the parenting plan, the asset exchange or liquidation, and financial support is easily agreed upon, which leaves a remainder part that becomes part of a different struggle — a different game. This is the part that triggers the oscillation between cooperation and competition I referred to earlier. How they finish up their resolution depends on a number of factors, including the emotional state of their relationship, psychological styles, past experiences in their relation and with others, their overall financial and career status, and the like. Some folks become high conflict and competitive when they become anxious. Others have residual connection and positive attachment to each other that drives cooperative motivation. Still others see the personal benefit of cooperation, which tends toward a mutual and constructive solution.

Let us make a couple of comments about the communication issue. In a zero-sum or zero-sum part of a game, the communication issue is not a significant factor other than the intent to express the type of game that is being played. I will now explain why by referring to a version of the PDG that divorcing spouses play. In the other part of the game, the cooperative, non-zero-sum part, communication plays a larger role. In fact, sometimes communication can move the game from a competitive dynamic to a cooperative dynamic. In the PDG that I referred to earlier, when the thieves are separated into two interrogation rooms they are precluded from any form of communication. Unless there are circumstances that justify absolute trust, there is a condition of uncertainty, which is precisely that which fuels distrust, along with the tendency toward defection and an oscillation of protection and competition.

Communication does not usually occur in a zero-sum game, especially when parties only choose once, and often even if it is an ongoing game. They usually know what each other's best moves are, and therefore communication is viewed as a waste of time or a weakening of one's interests. On the other hand, in mediation the goal is productive communication—a great deal of it. Good mediators know this and try to facilitate the free flow of communication and information exchange. They do this because more conversation often results in the discovery of alternative and sub-alternatives that were not considered earlier. Within my conceptual division between zero-sum and non-zero-sum aspects, the same principle applies. In these cases there are the parts of agreement, the parts of disagreement that are talked about, and the parts of disagreement about which there is no discussion. It is this last part in which a skilled mediator can make a significant difference. This is not to say that a mediation process can result in complete agreement, but it is academic that conversation tends toward more possible agreement.

Let's apply this way of thinking to the two thieves PDG hypothetical. Recall that in the scenario they are separated into different interrogation rooms. This prevents them from talking with each other, which they could utilize as a way to create more options. We can easily see how impossible it is to create more value in such a transaction if the parties cannot or do not speak with each other. In this case, it one can always improve one's position, i.e., external circumstances, by defecting from the agreement. This is so because neither thief can predict the other's behavior. Of course, this way of thinking does not take into account any value one achieves by keeping one's agreements, being virtuous, and the like. We can see, therefore, how easy it is to stay in a zero-sum dynamic if there is no free flow of information or dialogue. In contrast, if the thieves could speak with each other, especially in private, they could co-analyze their situation, and perhaps move the dynamic to a non-zero-sum game in which they both keep their agreement, thereby walking away with a manageable three months in jail for each.

This applies to divorce mediation situations, as well. I leave out of discussion a non-mediated divorce situation because these are usually hotly contested, zero-sum, winner-takes-all situations in which the spouses do not talk to each other anymore except through adversarial mouthpieces. In divorce mediation, the parties are somewhat situated like the thieves — more or less — except that no one prevents them from talking to each other than themselves except for themselves. In most divorce mediation cases there is a dialectical tension between defection and cooperation for both spouses. Defection is a natural human tendency towards self-protection, which is exacerbated by fear, anxiety, and uncertainty. Cooperation is a higher-order cognitive and moral state in which reflection overcomes anxiety. This leads to mutual benefit agreements that create more trust and therefore more fuel for complete and final resolution. It is the case that the more the parties rationally and mutually discuss their co-options, the greater the chance that they will resolve their case.

Let's take a look at the hypothetical we have been discussing. Using patience and driving the spouses to the bargaining table so to speak, the mediator was able to facilitate their sharing of anxieties. Then, after a few joint appointments, a curious phenomenon started occurring: the mediator noticed that there was a shifting attitude in conversation. The wife suggested she get a part-time job to pay part of her bills, which pleased her husband immensely. In return, he suggested that he pay her an amount of spousal support that would be based in part on actual salary, and in part based on bonuses actually received. She could see the reasoning in this and readily agreed. This enabled them to easily split the assets, and move on to an emotionally more challenging issue, the parenting plan. Eventually, the husband was able to be honest about the actual time he would have for their child, and then agreed to memorialize this in writing. The divorce soon finalized. Now let's move to the next chapter, in which I introduce additional concepts and ideas that will enrich the exploration.

Chapter 5

Transforming into a Non-Zero-Sum Game

Let's add some additional concepts to our discussion, address a few cases, and start looking at how we can use game theory to move a dynamic from zero-sum to non-zero-sum. Here a few case variations: In the DKS case the husband started the process in a very aggressive fashion though he purported to be cooperative. His spouse was stressed out and communicated repeatedly how surprised she was by the divorce. She would always follow up by stating that she wanted to get through it quickly and move on. In the PBD case, right from the beginning, the husband drafted a settlement plan to which he was committed. Any ideas from his spouse during the mediation process were met with significant resistance even though eventually he begrudgingly relented in order to get through the process.

In the CR case, the parties continuously stalled the mediation by taking far too long to bring required information into the negotiation; then they would blame the other, the mediator, or the process itself for delays and added costs. Finally, in the VJO case, it became apparent that the wife was playing the fence, seemingly cooperating in mediation albeit slowly while constructing her an adversarial, zero-sum approach in case the mediation did not work out. It was apparent that either she was not confident about the mediation or that she wasn't in it in good faith from the beginning. Eventually, her anxiety won out and she forced the case out of mediation. In all of these cases, the initiating (or lead) spouse led with a non-zero approach even though they claimed to be cooperative. This, of course, necessitated an ample educational phase in the beginning, which in some cases makes no difference if at least one of the parties cannot trust a cooperative process because of the vulnerabilities involved.

In a zero-sum dynamic the parties always pre-pick their strategies and do not consult the other when they do so. These come from anxiety, personality, and one's general hermeneutic stance in the world. What is interesting is that the parties can quickly become rooted in false beliefs about what they think are better ways to proceed. Equally interesting is that they often have stereotypical beliefs about how their spouses will respond—beliefs that are often false. Thus, regarding the cases above, in the DKS case the husband had false beliefs about the laws; in the PBD case the husband was so hermetically sealed and focused on the financial dimension that he had a hard time negotiating anything; in the CR case, both parties were unclear about what they actually wanted. Finally, in the VJO case, one of the spouses lacked a commitment to a non-zero-sum approach, which was fatal to mediation. All these false beliefs drove anxiety, which in turn, drove aggression or confusion.

In our main case that I presented earlier regarding the couple that was moving out of state, in the beginning of the mediation, both parties were closed off from each other and wanted a resolution that comported with stereotypical ways they saw each other, ways they saw divorce, and ways that they imagined their future. These perceptions were also driven by their personal histories, their childhoods, and the ways they learned to deal with conflict a long time before they met each other. They were pleasant enough with each other but this did not translate into a mutual agreement to play a non-zero-sum game. There are a number of responses to the situation in which a couple is not clearly in a cooperative mode. An important point to make, however, is that it is rare that both parties are fully cooperative or fully adversarial. Part of this truth comes from the nature of the situation. There is not just one choice to make as in the PDG; instead, there are several choices to make in an evolving and changing dynamic. Another part of this truth is psychological: depending upon the changing factors, both internal and external, parties oscillate from a higher-order cooperative motive to a protective, self-interested, defensive orientation. Higher order thinking comes when parties relax their anxiety, which allows them to see more mutual-benefit possibilities; limbic, fight or flight responses comes when anxiety and fear are high, and they are always adversarial, by way of passivity or aggressivity. One of the artistic aspects of being a mediator is to deftly work within this oscillation.

So let's now move forward in the deepening of our discussion. I have addressed the issue of communication in a brief way, although I believe that a full-length study of these issues in mediation would be valuable and important. However, there are other issues I'd like to broach. One of them is the issue involving who goes first in a divorce. That is, it is often the case that there is an initiator and a follower with regard to the court filings. It is often the case that one of the parties makes first contact with mediation, and therefore leads in this aspect as well. The other party is the follower, and in many cases, only learns about the divorce after the initiator speaks with a mediator or lawyer. For other parties who follow, they do so intentionally, believing that they have more power and control by allowing the initiator to make the first move, from beginning to end. Either these parties become full participants in the process and take some initiative, or eventually they lead the process into litigation.

Let's look a little further into the issue of the order of making choices. Recall that in a typical divorce mediation process, there are typical items to negotiate, including spousal support, the separation of property and money, sometimes a small business ownership and income, and a parenting plan. Someone leads the negotiation process, perhaps in each of the different areas, and perhaps only in some. Making the first offer in a particular area shows one hand, to be sure, leaving one without bargaining room if they have given too much in the beginning. On the other hand, if it is a fair offer, it can set initial parameters, which influences the other party's response (and this influence in a mediation is presumably cooperative and mutual). In our examples, we can see how easy it is for one party to be aggressive, trying to force the transaction in a certain direction. However, the emotional aspect of aggression affects many people in one of two ways: one, it can cause an individual to withdraw from fully participating, which is counter-productive because there is a lack of commitment to any sort of deal making; or two, it can cause the second party to become aggressive, which tends toward a zero-sum dynamic.

Nevertheless, as long as the parties are both truly oriented toward a non-zero-sum approach, the order of choices and events is less important. For example, in any of the cases I mentioned above, if the initiating or leading party approached the other in a cooperative way, this would have reduced anxiety and opened a mutual problem-solving expectation. This is usually reducible to communication style, word choice, overall intent, and the like, in which the initiator speaks with invitations rather than mandates or inflexible dynamics. If this occurs, both parties feel autonomous, empowered, in control of their own participation, and less anxious with the outcome.

Another feature of divorce negotiation in mediation contexts is the dual problem of lack of control over a changing world and a continuous lack of full information. Even though both parties in mediation commit to full disclosure of all pertinent and relevant information, lives can change quickly, and new facts can emerge quickly. To be sure, in adversarial contexts, some individuals are tempted to withhold information that would give both parties equal bargaining power. This approach, however, erodes autonomy, trust, and mutuality, and only leads to a zero-sum dynamic. If, however, the parties always share important information in a timely way, this ensures the development of trust, along with mutual benefit agreements that result in win-win outcomes. When some unpredictable event from the outside world occurs this can drive both parties to increased anxiety. When this involves one of the parties, this effect is magnified. Therefore, we can see how this factor significantly effects the oscillation between cooperation and competition. A good mediation process is sensitive to this factor and constantly encourages the parties to expect change, and to share information on an ongoing basis with accuracy and comprehensiveness.

Sometimes either one of the parties, even though cooperative, can become anxious about a particular issue, and deal with it by engaging in a closure process. This process can involve various strategies that reframe the situation as a small set of polarized alternatives with various pressures brought to bear on the choices. In these cases, the other party has to deal with this anxiety in terms of passivity, aggressivity, or mutuality. Even for those individuals who do not initiate these closures, it is easy for them to be hooked by them and to respond accordingly. These responses, however, drive the mediation toward litigation. On the other hand, if a party does not attach to these hooks, he or she has an opportunity to drive the dynamic back toward mutuality. All this can be accomplished with effective mediation and communication that opens discussion without raising anxiety. At some point in negotiations, both parties will want to crystallize their agreements, into a set of mutual benefit agreements that are formalized in writing; however, this is different from anxiety-based closures that often occur in the beginning and middle of the process. We shall soon see that these are opportunities for a qualified mediator to reopen mutuality and therefore a wider number of solution sets to the parties' different needs and preferences.

Another issue that we can contemplate involves the number of iterations of the negotiation there will be. Frequently, in marital dissolution, if the spouses do not have children, and especially if one of them will be moving out of town, the situation will be viewed as one-time negotiation. From a purely game theoretical perspective, then, the parties will have no analytic motivation beyond the outcome of that one and only negotiation. Thus, self-interest is at a premium, and cooperation is likely only in terms of that self-interest. The only exception occurs when the parties have evolved senses of compassion, empathy, leftover sympathies, and/ or evolved moral conscience. In the case of an exception, the parties, realizing that it is a one-time negotiation, are motivated toward a fair outcome that goes beyond personal interest. If the parties do not have these empathic tendencies then the transaction tends toward a negotiation that is based on self-interest. This is usually a sufficient reason for the parties to cooperate lest they end up with a result that is analogous to both prisoners going to prison for 6 years in the PDG. In divorce this means that the parties litigate their issues, spend a great deal of money in legal fees, destroy any possibilities of remaining friendly and socially civil, and the like. In contrast, there is the case of an indefinite number of iterations of the negotiation, which usually involves co-parenting, joint properties the parties wish to retain, or some social/professional co-interest, at least until they reach a complete settlement or resolution in the future. In this case, at a very minimum, the parties cooperate with each other because they have common interests. However, when resolution looks imminent, sometime in the future, the negotiation may start to transform into the one-time scenario. Competent mediation takes these dynamics into consideration, facilitating their illumination and discussion, which tends toward a higher degree of sustainability.

There are additional problems that I will discuss in an introductory way in the balance of this chapter. They include side payments, rationality, the unconscious, personality, and Nash Equilibrium. I also reiterate that these considerations are not exhaustive, but I intend them to stimulate further thinking by mediation practitioners; we also intend to discuss them more deeply in future work. This is to say that theory and ideals often regulate thinking and practice, but it is also the case that real life scenarios deviate in well-defined ways from them. For example, it is usually the case that the parties are not that rational; or that they experience unconscious phenomena that interfere with clear, logical thinking.

It can be the case that the mediator is not fully aware of all the aspects of a mediation process. Sometimes there is communication that occurs outside of the mediation process that involves hidden or side agreements. Usually these involve items that the parties prefer to be confidential for legal, sexual, or even practical reasons. Occasionally, they are aspects of the mediation that the parties actually don't disagree about but which they prefer to keep hidden. Sometimes these agreements operate as a factor in the mediation, but when a mediator isn't aware of them, except intuitively, this can disrupt the process. This raises the suggestion of full transparency, not just between the parties, but also between the parties and the mediator. Remember, we are trying to clarify and understand the dialectic between zero-sum and non-zero-sum dynamics, and we must consider any factor, known or unknown, that affects them. Let's continue our discussion about the factors of rationality, personality, the unconscious, Nash Equilibrium, and in passing, any other factor that can affect the negotiation. Later in this book I will explore my new interpretation of the PDG, which challenges rationality, the autonomous fully aware subject, and the possibility of equilibrium.

Rational thinking is at the very basis of game theory, which implies that a party will always act thoughtfully and will not reject reasonable solutions. It assumes that human behavior is guided by instrumental reason and that individuals always choose what they believe to be the best means to achieve their ends. This system of pursuing preferences in the best ways possible is utilitarian; figuring out each party's utilities can go a long way toward resolution. We can see in this way of thinking that it assumes that people know their preferences, the best ways of attaining them, and that they fully appreciate all the choices that are possible. If this were true, parties to a negotiated dispute would have more ability to predict outcomes of various choice sets, and perhaps this would lead to a greater frequency of resolutions. However, most senior mediators know that so-called "rationality" is an elusive ideal for a number of reasons, which I will address her summarily.

The first problem is that each person has her own subjective system of valuation. For example, a divorcing spouse may be willing to "pay" thousands of dollars for a piece of furniture worth $500 if it has sentimental value. While it is true that systems of subjective values often converge in various ways, it is equally true that a portion of the transaction often becomes idiosyncratic. On this point, some parents trade off time with children for reduced spousal support. A second problem is that because parties often have extreme differences in values — which is partially responsible for the dissolution — the way they interpret rationality can often vary. What seems irrational to outsiders, including a mediator, might be perfectly rational to a party. For example, sometimes parties become tired with the divorce process and pay off various fees, costs, and expenses that their spouses refuse to pay — in order to move on with their lives. Some of us might counsel to put up a bigger fight, or to be patient, but upon reflection we can see how these individuals value their time and mental wellbeing. For them, these moves are highly rational.

There additional issues associated with the assumption of rationality. At best, most of us are emotional beings even when we have problems to solve. These emotions frame how we see these conflict situations and can both hinder our thinking but also make it more consonant with our preferences. It is the debilitating effects of emotion, however, about which we should be concerned. For example, anger or fear can severely affect our ability to reason; for this reason, highly skilled mediation can correct distortions in thinking due to intense feelings. The main point is, nevertheless, that substantial emotions erode the idea of pure rationality.

There are stronger forms of the same phenomena, which involve personality, trauma, erroneous thinking, self-deception, and the unconscious motivations of behavior. It is helpful to understand that in the European Enlightenment we actually believed in the idea of mental autonomy, methodologies of rational thinking, and the like. It was true at that time, that we didn't conceptualize the powerful effects of the unconscious in which we house trauma and pathology. Poor judgment and self-deception were thought to be correctable through the right method and/or the right counsel. There is a vast literature that explores subjectivity, especially in terms of these distortions. There is another literature—what we call critical theory—that suggests there is something like a cultural unconscious; this, we can see, contains invisible and difficult-to-discern phenomena that structuralize what we take to be rational in the first place. In short, rationality is a very important topic that we must examine further, for it is at the foundation of game theory.

Let's take another look at the Prisoner's Dilemma Game (PDG), and include discussion of Nash Equilibrium and Pareto Optimal. Let us not forget that in some cases, divorce is a single transaction that the parties will never play again with each other. In these cases, there is a strong tendency to cooperate—within certain subjective rational bounds—in order to quickly move on to a new life. However, if these bounds are crossed and there is little to no lingering sympathy and empathy, the parties can be tempted to play a zero-sum game; in these cases, moving to win-win dynamic is unmotivated and the parties will fight to the end to win. In other cases, which are almost completely cooperative, in which there isn't much to fight about, the parties quite easily move toward a cooperative and efficient ending process. The third group of cases, in which there is some complexity, and at least one substantive area to quarrel about, moving toward a win-win dynamic is more difficult and may depend largely on whether there will be some ongoing relation or not. We would then have a situation of n-iterations, the indefiniteness of which creates space for cooperation. Incidentally, over time this cooperation usually creates feelings of trust, sympathy, and empathy as the parties dissolve their relationship in a more gradual way over time.

If we look at the original facts of the PDG, it appears initially as a rational choice theory; if so, the conclusion is obvious: one must defect on the agreement by giving testimony against the other thief. Part of the strength of the dilemma is its context. The two men are criminals, up to no good, and therefore we tend to overlook the moral dimension—the dimension of loyalty and only focus on one dimension, which involves getting out of jail or prison time. However, when we shift the story to other contexts such as divorce, we open up interpretive space for a different view of the moral dimension. The new context sets up a whole new moral world for most individuals, even those who are angry at one another. There are social customs and etiquette therefore that constrict the behavior of the parties to a range of acceptability. In viewing the PDG in purely "rational" terms, we can easily conclude that the correct answer is always to defect. However, when we add the inevitable ethical dimension to the equation, what is considered rational becomes more complex. Let's look at this further.

In the typical presentation of the PDG, each party has a narrowly framed sort of self-interest, and that is to stay out of jail or prison. Thus, the "Good" is interpreted only in these terms except for a moral domain that is not usually included in the discussion. For example, the parties could have a loyalty and solidarity toward each other that would preclude ever intentionally harming each other. In that case it wouldn't matter what interrogators told either one, for they simply would not offer testimony against other. Purists might still argue that the most rational choice is to defect from the agreement of silence, and framed in those terms they would be correct. However, this is a skewed and distorted view of humanity and human nature. When we shift the context, however, to marital dissolution, a context that is in principle law abiding, moral, and so forth—at least in most cases—this moral dimension becomes more salient and pronounced.

It is not only the interpersonal dyad that is important here; it also includes the overarching worldview of most communities with which we are familiar, and therefore it necessarily includes the moral. This can be further refined into a duty of fairness even though the parties are splitting up and may never speak to one another again. Nevertheless, and this is the tricky part, it would not be rational to assume that the other party will value goodwill and fairness in this situation; even so, it is still arguable more rational to offer goodwill, fairness, and cooperation to the other party. This is the only possible way a non-zero-sum outcome can happen. We can see, though, how these dynamics can easily lead to oscillations between cooperation and competition even amongst individuals who value both rationality and fairness. This implies that there are internal goods, such as virtuous behavior, that can weigh in considerations of rationality. People who get divorced most often value these internal goods, especially when they self-select for the cooperative, non-zero-sum approach of mediation.

Another issue that emerges often involves the motivation of one of the parties to "beat" his or her spouse, even in cooperative conditions, intending that his or her own payoff is secondary to the main goal. For example, a number of parties will overspend professional fees as part of their goal to feel like they have won something from their spouses. This can obviously become irrational if these additional expenses easily outweigh benefits, but it is a deeply emotional and relational issue that tests the idea of rationality. Another example we can across recently was a spouse who refused to sell out his share of the marital home to the other spouse and in so doing paralyzed the process, which increased stress and professional fees. This is, in some ways, akin to the "final iteration" dynamic in which even highly cooperative parties fail to cooperate in the final stages of the process once they realize that there will not be an ongoing relationship. This can derail a divorce process, and can also create undue stress in co-parenting arrangements even years after the final dissolution date.

Before we end this section by reviewing Nash Equilibrium and looking at Pareto Optimization, I want to make some miscellaneous comments about rationality. We are all somewhat controlled by our own history and our own unconscious self. It is difficult to become aware of these forces that move us to action. It is equally difficult to understand our own personalities, and how they act as interpretive filters for all of our experience. For both of these factors, the unconscious and the personality, we have to engage in deep introspection to gain any perspective about them. This is not to say that a good mediation process cannot facilitate this learning process, but it can be difficult if one has not done much of this work prior to divorce mediation. A related consider is whether one ought to employ the tit-for-tat strategy in a mediation process, that is to say, start with cooperation and follow the other party in his moves. Thus, if the other cooperates you would cooperate and so forth. This can be an effective strategy, but we should also consider an alternative of always cooperating even when the other defects. This can create trust and equilibrium, which can lead to a stronger foundation for a cooperative resolution, especially in divorce.

Pareto optimization is an allocation of goods or resources such that improving any one party's position any further would result in a loss for the other party. It is a principle of efficiency that recognizes that there are points of distribution beyond which we cannot go without someone losing a good or a resource. The principle is not concerned with fairness in any way, so while the parties may be able to optimize an allocation in divorce this does not mean it is fair. Thus, it is true that fairness—as expressed by legal considerations—acts as a constraint to some optimization choices. In contrast, Nash Equilibrium occurs where both parties have chosen a strategy and neither can change position—individually—without further loss in position. It is an example of equilibrium because neither side would independently change position for the worse. Let's see how it works in the PDG.

Recall that there are four variations in the dilemma, represented as different outcomes. In three of them a party can improve his position by changing his mind and defecting. However, the fourth variation, in which both parties have already chosen to defect and each get six years in prison, is an example of Nash Equilibrium. This is the case, because if either party changes position he will get nine years in prison instead of six. We'd like to think that both parties would have such a degree of loyalty and cooperation that they would get together on strategy and leave jail after three months, but they don't decide together; they decide individually. What is more is that because they have been separated into different interrogation rooms (and presumably threatened), they cannot reassure each other of their loyalty and commitment to the agreement.

A similar logic applies in Puccini's famous opera, Tosca, as well as in mediated divorces. Because of the anxiety, stress, and uncertainty in dividing assets, determining spousal and/or child support, and drafting a co-parenting plan, the parties are tempted to defect on any implied or explicit agreement to cooperate subject to legal bounds of fairness. To the extent that they cannot trust each other, the process heads toward unsavory Nash Equilibrium where both parties defect in some way. This drives up fees, stress, creates ongoing animosity, and makes co-parenting difficult. Unfortunately, at the very heart of the divorce is often a lack of trust, so it can be challenging to produce it in a cooperative divorce. However, if a creative and thoughtful mediation can facilitate a Nash Equilibrium that both parties prefer then neither will be tempted to defect. An additional strategy is to render the mediation voidable if one party defects (and then carefully define "defect"). Let's take a look at some games that can help us understand how to create Equilibrium in mediated settlements.

Chapter 6

Introduction to Additional Games & Better Communication

While it is true that all divorcing spouses play the Prisoner's Dilemma Game, we can also look at the PDG itself as contextual worldview—as the paradigm for life and for this sort of strategic situation of divorce—within which a number of other games can be played. Let's look at some of these games in the context of divorce. The first one that comes to mind is the cake-cutting situation in which one spouse offers a partial deal, for example, to buy the other out of the family house. To make this into a cake-cutting scenario, the spouse who presents the transaction would need to make the deal work in both directions: either spouse could buy out the other on the same terms. The point is that most people have strong intuitions about fairness and the cake-cutting exercise insures it. However, to be clear, the cake-cutting exercise is an example of the minimax strategy, which only applies to zero-sum situations. Divorce mediation, most often tends toward non-zero-sum dynamic—with some distortions. The cake-cutting method, which is a fair division process, can be applied with great success to some parts of a mediation process as long as they are separable. For example, the parties may easily agree to a fair division with regard to assets while hotly disputing the parenting plan. A type of this method can easily occur with regard to spousal or child support in a number of jurisdictions that have a statutory calculator. This operates as a third party, authoritative standard, insures fairness, and can often take the conflict out of part of the process.

Another game spouses can play in a divorce, at least with regard to a portion of it, is chicken. This usually occurs in "mediations" that are not entered into in good faith by one party who plays at least two games. This sort of a party enters into mediation but simultaneously prepares for litigation. As such, there is no real non-zero-sum dynamic, the truth of which eventually emerges. Playing chicken, which is a game of brinkmanship, is like two cars headed toward each other. The first car to swerve out of the way loses. In divorce, one spouse usually offers a take it or leave proposition, in at least one area of the dissolution. This creates fear and anxiety in the second spouse, decreases trust, but can be masked by clever communication tactics. In a sense it is a sort of bribe, or side payment, and is usually intended to operate outside of the main mediation process. It is a good example of how non-transparent communications can destroy a good mediation.

In a pure game of chicken both spouses agree to enter into it. In contrast, in an unexecuted game, one party plays it, thereby inviting the other to enter, but this does not always occur. Another alternative way to frame this invitation is as an ultimatum, which sometimes occurs when one party feels afraid or stressed. It is important to stress that this type of situation is at the core of mediation. In this situation there is an oscillation between cooperation and competition whereby there are parts of the mediation that contain non-zero-sum dynamics, but other parts that are excluded because of strong feelings. Realistically, this can occur when both parties have some cooperative elements but who are both willing to fight it out on certain issues. By "swerving" toward each other each party avoids driving his or her car off the road into certain fatal accident. Thus, there are two Nash Equilibrium points here because either party would want to avoid driving off the road.

The best outcome, of course, is for both parties to opt out of the game of chicken, and look at some better mutual strategies. A variation of the game occurs when the consequence of swerving is not fatal or disastrous but is inconvenient or not preferred. This is often the case in divorce, and it is usually resolved open the negotiations to other goods, and then trading. For example, if both parties are in a game of chicken, one of them can switch out this game for one that is more mutually preferable by adding new elements. That is, fighting over the parenting plan can be resolved by looking at the mediation agreement as a whole. This dissolves the anxiety and provides real chances for a Nash Equilibrium that is fair and mutually preferential.

Another game is the "woe is me" or "self pity" game. This is a distortion in thinking, a self-deception that causes a party to not see reality. This creates blockades in a win-win mediation process because at a deep level it creates an unequal dynamic. An alternate articulation of this game is that it sets up a perpetrator-victim role-playing sort of communication in which the victim is "due" more than his or her fair share in the mediation. Although there may be some elements of unfairness in the relationship, this is often the case for couples that seek divorce, and they are rarely only one-sided dynamics. Like chicken, it is born of anxiety and alienates the parties from a mutual, non-zero-sum dynamic at least with regard to this part of the negotiations. Usually when one of the parties plays this game, the other party plays a corresponding one, usually of the same ilk but with a different language. Here is an example: one of the parties accuses her spouse of various forms of emotional abuse; in contrast, her husband accuses her of stealing money and taking advantage of him in various ways, including threats about removing the children from him. If played right, this game usually attracts the sympathy of outsiders, court personnel, and inattentive mediators. However, everyone soon sees the complex impasse, and a good mediation environment can break through to a more productive dynamic.

Sometimes if one party proposes the "woe is me game" it is often in response to the dictator game. In the dictator game, which happens quite often, one of the parties constructs a wholesale proposal that he or she offers to the other, expecting agreement or disagreement as a whole. This occurs quite often in the early stages of a marital dissolution process and can be coupled with a version of the game of chicken or the ultimatum game. We can also see that the second party is expected to play a passive position, although this never happens in a pure way. Good mediation can bring the parties together in a mutual problem-solving way that is assertive and neither passive nor aggressive. Two additional games worth mentioning are the "stalling game" and the "complexifying game." Both are attempts to manipulate the dynamic away from mutuality toward various domination strategies. Stalling attempts to tire the other party in order to gain an advantage. Making a transaction more complex often creates confusion to the benefit of the party creating it. What I have relayed may not be an exhaustive list of games but they are illustrative of the types of unproductive and distortive dynamics with which parties start mediation processes. Let's now deepen our discussion about transforming these distorted dynamics toward a more mutual, non-zero-sum game with good outcomes for both parties.

There are behavioral, non-verbal, and verbal strategies to bring a dynamic more into alignment with win-win possibilities for both parties. Of course, the first step is to recognize the game that the other party is playing. Obviously if it is cooperative we ought to give the other party positive acknowledgment that this is the kind of productive and constructive behavior that will lead to beneficial outcomes for both. Much has been written about the importance of communication for successful mediation, but I'd like to make a few points relative to the game theory dimension. In general, verbal communication is better than no or little communication. Usually, a lack of communication is an earmark for a zero-sum dynamic in which the parties fight it out to see who can dominate the other. When they communicate, however, they open up possibilities to redesign their dispute as a cooperative one. Yet, it must go further: the type of communication must be reward based, express honest needs and preferences, and allow for compromise.

At the beginning of a negotiation, especially in the context of divorce, each party has his or her own private fantasies about what a good result looks like. These fantasies are designed to minimize stress and anxiety. When two parties start discussing divorce processes, property allocations, spousal and child maintenance, and the like, the other party's interests collide, thereby elevating anxiety. This is at the level of the fight or flight limbic, instinctual response. The mediation process challenges these anxieties, allowing for the parties to see that not only can their interests coincide they can actually create more resources together than by contest. This process usually creates the conditions for a mutually cooperative result—one that overcomes all of the games that I mentioned earlier. In short, most of the games that parties play in divorce are self-protective in kind but in reality actually detract from their self-interest, and the interests of everyone else involved.

In addition to cooperative strategies, zero-sum strategies tend toward derailed mediation and eventual litigation. However, parties often play either a minimally cooperative strategy or a mixed strategy. In later volumes of this book series we will investigate some of the underlying mathematics, but ultimately we will see that mixed strategies and minimally cooperative strategies oscillate between competition and cooperation. Another way to say this is that rational, self-caring individuals always monitor their best alternative to a negotiated settlement. When negotiations become frayed there are natural tendencies to consider this best alternative. When negotiations go well most people put that best alternative on the shelf and do not think about it much. Further, we have found that to the extent the parties negotiate cooperative solutions they optimize their resources, i.e., their utility functions. To the extent that the parties compete with adversarial dynamics they decrease the amount of resources available to split.

The essential element to this optimizing process, one in which anxieties are conquered and zero-sum dynamics are transcended, is the building of trust. This does not mean that the parties will ever trust each other like perhaps they did when they were well married and happy, but it does mean that they can trust each other to cooperate—to some level—in a mediation that optimizes their separating resources. It doesn't mean they like each other; it doesn't mean they sympathize with each other, but it does mean that they follow the law, behave with moral sensitivity, and reflect carefully in a way that results in resource optimization.

A lack of trust moves negotiations toward a zero-sum process that becomes stressful, more distrustful, less kind, and highly adversarial. These cases inevitably move toward litigation and a lack of optimization of resources follows. In contrast, the building of trust leads to a cooperative dynamic and a constellation of optimized or nearly optimized solutions. This process starts with an education about the difference between cooperative and competitive strategies so that the parties develop a mentalization of the difference. Then, once the parties fully commit to a cooperative process, thereby creating anxiety and vulnerability, they can enter into low-risk, mutual-benefit agreements. If they are both reliable and follow these agreements they create a predictable sense of trust. To be sure, there is almost always a penumbra of anxiety, but it can be largely overcome by mutual follow-through with these agreements. These follow-throughs create a sense that risk can be averted and another sense that cooperation will pay off better than other strategies. It is also true that if either party defects early by violating their interim agreements, trust does not build and any that already had is gone sometimes for the duration of the process.

This involves the problem of who makes the first, trusting-trustworthy move. Far too often, the process is paralyzed because neither party will make the first good faith offer of some kind for fear that the offer would be too much. However, making the first offer about some aspect of the negotiation, perhaps a concession of some sort, start the series of choices with one that is cooperative. This creates a psychological propensity in the other party to respond in kind. Furthermore, if this sort of interim agreement is made in writing it has a formalized symbolism. It registers as serious and credible. For most people this also operates as a mechanism that creates an impetus not to violate the offer. For example, in a divorce mediation process, one of the parties might make an offer about co-parenting that he or she would be willing to put in writing, as a good faith way to create credibility and trust; this sets the tempo and expectation for the next steps.

The initial point is that one of the parties must go first in the negotiation. This is a very powerful opportunity to create a cooperative expectation by making a clear initial commitment, the violation of which would destroy the foundation of mediation. A second strategy is to outline a method or set of steps to which both parties agree at least in principle. Of course it is important to keep the system flexible but usually the parties feel a sense of trust when they mutually create an expectation—a path to follow. A third strategy involves a memorialization of an interim or partial agreements; even though they are part of a mediation process and confidential, these writings add a solemnity that usually creates trust. This trust opens opportunities to co-create win-win outcomes. A fourth strategy (and I am sure there are more) is to initiate trust by being generous and accommodating from the outset. This has a tendency to re-ignite pair-bonding feelings of altruism that are left over from the better days of the marriage. It also expresses an intention create goodwill in the future.

Another strategy to keep the process moving in a cooperative and productive direction is to play the tit for tat game. This follows from making an initial cooperative move; the next move is determined by whether the other person is cooperative or adversarial and should match it. Thus, if a first spouse is initially cooperative and the second is uncooperative and adversarial, the first spouse should respond in kind to match the nature of the choice. This has the logic of reciprocity, which is started by a cooperative and constructive move and a matching move. This either leads to a cooperative mediation or an adversarial litigation depending upon the pattern of choices and behaviors by both parties. In short, it would be foolhardy and unrealistic for one party to continue cooperating when the other party continuously defects. On the other hand, if the parties are in a confused retaliatory pattern, it is incumbent upon one of them to break it by interceding with a new, cooperative behavior. This creates the best possibilities for a positive and constructive resolution. A good mediator can help this by facilitating repeated interactions, present and future, and by keeping both parties aware of their mutual goals and the mission of mediation.

Finally, I'd like to make a few comments about the strategy of creating Nash Equilibrium. This is the situation in which a party cannot escape from or defect from an agreement without experiencing loss of some kind. This actually happens often in mediation, for example, when the parties create co-parenting agreements or decide property transfers and spousal maintenance payments. Once finally agreed to, a defection would normally put that party in a worse position—this is Nash Equilibrium. Let's put some facts on the table. Divorcing husband and wife agree to $2,000 monthly support for the wife, statutory child support, a 60%-40% time split with the two children (in favor of the wife), and a complicated distribution of house, vehicles, art, and miscellaneous home items. Because the wife was going to take most of these items, she agreed to the $2,000 support instead of the $2,300 monthly support that the statutory calculator would have given her. Then the husband started dating a new woman during the mediation process, which his wife was very upset about when she heard of it. In this case they had achieved Nash Equilibrium—a go-forward resolution that would finish their case in a good way. However, the presence of the new romantic partner upset this homeostasis: the wife withdrew her agreement on spousal support, and the household items were eventually equally shared to the wife's dismay. This eventually de-stabilized the process further, which resulted in the wife/mother losing more agreed-upon time with her children. In future volumes, we will explore this equilibrium with more trenchant detail.

Chapter 7

Two Case Studies

We have so far described what game theory is and how it can be helpful to not only make sense of decision-making in divorce situations but to also enhance the rationality of the parties for better mutual outcomes. We have looked at the distinction between zero-sum and non-zero-sum games, how parties never have complete information, and the Prisoner's Dilemma as paradigm for this strategic and highly emotional life phase. We have mentioned that sometimes the parties play mixed strategies, cooperating in part and competing otherwise, and in various ways trying to dominate the process. We have looked at a few additional games such as chicken, stalling, complexifying, and self-pity games. We have discussed maximin and minimax principles, Pareto Optimization, and Nash Equilibrium, amongst others. We have also discussed the value of careful communication as a way of converting a dynamic from an adversarial, zero-sum process into a cooperative, non-zero-sum dynamic. There are may other concepts, but we will leave them for another volume. For now, let's take what we have learned and apply it to a couple of marital dissolution cases. This will show more specifically how we can use game theory to the divorce mediation scenario.

The following hypothetical case, which we will call the "Betterman" case, is an example of a long-term marriage with assets and minor children, debts, and claims for spousal and children support. I will next delineate some of the facts of the matter, and then proceed to discuss the difference between a cooperative, mediated solution and an adversarial, litigated solution. By using some of the introductory and basic concepts in game theory, we can begin to see its usefulness in decision-making, and in the communication between professional and clients.

The case initially came to the mediator with a phone call from a spouse who had been recently served process by his wife, who was asking for spousal and child support, half of the assets, and attorney's fees. She had engaged an attorney, her husband was living part-time with his girlfriend, and the dynamic was contentious. Clearly, the case was starting with predominantly adversarial, zero-sum dynamics although through conversation we learned that both spouses still cared a great deal for each other and hoped they could be good co-parents. This case could have easily followed a litigated path. Here are some of the likely outcomes of the litigated path framed in terms of a basic game theory perspective.

By using the Prisoner's Dilemma framework as a working model, we can see that the wife had already defected from most of a cooperative model. She had already started to demonize her husband, and was making a play for a competitive share of the resources of the family and marital estate. The house was worth $1.5 million with 300,000 debt. They had joint credit cards totaling 60,000. He made over $250,000 annually with some bonus increases on top of that. She currently made nothing, but was expecting at least a 100,000 inheritance within a couple of years. There were two teenage minor children who planned to attend college. Finally, he had recently been to a series of doctors and as it turns out, needed to start winding down his professional work lest he expire from a heart attack or stroke. Moreover, they lived in a tightly knit community and had a number of acquaintances and friends in common.

Let's look at a likely adversarial, litigated path for this couple. If the husband hires an attorney and if mediation is not explored, the husband will end up moving out, so his time with his children will likely be constrained. Because there would be two professionals in the case who are ethically required to advocate for their respective clients, fees will quadruple or more. For sake of discussion, let's set total mediation fees at $10,000 – 20,000 and total litigation fees at $50,000 – 100,000. In addition, a well-mediated case would take 8 months total, including the statutory wait period. In contrast, their litigated case would take 2 years, requiring many more court appearances and lost time at work or with the children. Please keep in mind that I am over-simplifying the facts for sake of discussion, but these figures are not very far from the actual truth.

Chances are good that the husband would eventually move into a small apartment or move in with his girlfriend because of friction at home. Ironically his moving out would cause additional friction and we'd expect the wife to be upset with his bringing the children around his girlfriend. He would respond with comments about her large inheritance, perhaps initiating a blaming cycle, to which she would eventually respond. They would soon be in a mutual defection-mode of a Prisoner's Dilemma Game analogue that the attorneys would further entrench. Assuming attorneys nearly equal in ability, he parties would soon lose a cooperative solution and the money/resources they would be fighting over would mostly go to these attorneys.

In every case that chooses the competitive, adversarial root, there is always an intersection when the process forever shifts in this direction. At this point both parties leave their mutual, cooperative communication dynamic, and more fully commit to aggressive, dominating strategies such as chicken, stalling, complexifying, self-pity, and many others. The commonality is that they are aggressive and more importantly they move in a zero-sum, competitive direction. In principle these strategies do not optimize the joint preferences and resources of both parties, but actually decrease the sum of the resources available for allocation between them, and to the children. Moreover, even for the party who "wins," there is a loss because of substantial attorney's fees, costs, time out of work, stress, unfriendly co-parenting in the future (which adds to costs), and loss of other opportunities. In short, by defecting from obvious types of cooperation, both parties end up in an instance of Nash Equilibrium.

In this situation, because the parties have defected from the original cooperative plan, it is very difficult to shift the dynamic back in this direction—difficult but not impossible. More frequently, each party is in a situation in which any change in strategy results in further loss, which no one is likely to do. This actually happens often, where the parties have lost cooperative containment, are sitting in a Nash Equilibrium, and one of the parties suggests a new cooperative approach. In general, this does not happen. On occasion, they can enter into small, low-risk, cooperative agreements that potentially can drive the overall process back to a non-zero-sum dynamic but this is difficult and expensive because it takes more time. Furthermore, the presence of the attorneys, as proxies, seals the dynamic fate of the process in more cases than not.

Let's review. Even though they were still paying regular mortgage payments there was a market downturn coming, which could easily decrease the current FMV of the house. Statutory wait periods in some states are substantial: even six months can have a significant effect on the market value of a home, so time spent haggling can, in the end, result in a decrease of overall resources, like in this case. There was also a shake-up at the husband's company, which could result in a lost job, lost bonus, or some other loss in net pay. What made this worse was that he was experiencing chest pains, and his doctors cautioned him against further stress. This brings us to mounting credit card debt with substantial interest rates. The wife maintained her position that she had to focus herself on parenting their children for the next few years; then she would look for a job. This meant that part of the credit card payments would come out of her share of the marital estate; this, in turn, would further limit her housing possibilities. We can easily see even in this over-simplified hypothetical situation that an adversarial approach cascades into the ongoing and increasing losses in resources. Psychologically, the more loss they experienced the more they fought for what was left. There is much more to say here, and in future volumes to this work, we will present mathematical analysis; for now, however, let's move on to a commentary about a cooperative approach.

If the parties maintain a cooperative dynamic, they will not move out of their higher-level brain functioning that allows them the greatest degree of reflectivity and rationality. They will respect each other's choices about new friends and partners, and they will come to mutual agreements about interim and long-term co-parenting arrangements. They may employ a mediator to help them analyze and optimize their financial and property resources as well, not worrying about making an immediate decision, but moving through the process in a deliberate, thoughtful way. This kind of arrangement would greatly decrease their stress, and create trust between them for the future. In turn, this would ease the minds of their children, which would further regulate and limit any kind of potentially destructive energies.

Because there is trust between the divorcing spouses and their children feel safe; because there is a reflective and rational process; because they did not hire advocates who would quickly turn the dynamic into a zero-sum; and finally because they contained all of their anxious, aggressive energies within a kind and cooperative process, they had good chances for a cooperative resolution and a long-term co-parenting relationship. As such, the husband's health improved and the wife started considering a part-time job. In terms of the financial and material resources involved, they would be able to optimize their allocation, quickly sell their house (or arrange for the wife and kids to stay in it), and obtain a divorce with a modest mediation fee. Along the way, they would be able to discover new cooperative possibilities that they never thought possible.

Let's make a few more comments about this case now that we understand the difference between cooperative and competitive approaches. In terms of the PDG, they arrived a good enough result in which both parties received what they needed and most of what they preferred. Although it seems that either party could have gained if he or she had defected, a simple review of the PDG shows that this is not the case: the other party would have quickly realized the defection and would have tried to discuss the matter immediately. Often it is the case that a party will defect unconsciously; they do things that are motivated from repressed childhood trauma, and once aware of their behavior, are quickly able to transform it into cooperative approach. In this case, the parties' communication opened their process to new and better solutions rather than to close it as litigation would have done. Their mediator was able to facilitate the regulation of their anxieties to help keep them on track; once they trusted the process, it became easier as it moved forward.

Sometimes even parties who are mostly cooperative have divided internal motivations, which result in mixed strategies and occasional attempts at aggressive domination of the other in various regions of the negotiation. A good mediation process with kind communication between the parties can identify and regulate aggressive manifestations that arise during the process. As I have outlined in an earlier drafted, The Myth of Mediation Neutrality, we can better understand these hidden and mixed motivations by assuming that part of the mind is unconscious or less than conscious. Good mediation can challenge the resistant and intransigent aspects of adversarial dynamics and re-align them with a non-zero-sum approach. Now that we have discussed in a preliminary way a long-term marriage with children, let's discuss a second case study that involves a short-term marriage with substantial assets, no children, and international aspects.

In this situation the parties were married only three years. They had met in their home country of India at a business conference, and within six months had married. The husband took his new bride to the U.S. to live in his house. While his career was ascending, the new wife had trouble adjusting to American life or getting a job that met her expectations. The two tried to have children, unsuccessfully, and eventually their young marriage lost its charm. The husband then started a new relationship with someone else, and wanted out of his marriage as quickly as possible. Because the two spouses had common family friends and acquaintances back in their home country, especially the husband wanted to proceed in a discreet and careful way even though he had already embarrassed himself with the affair. Keep in mind that most of the money in the marriage was coming from the husband's $300,000/year job, although the wife received monies from her family. Also keep in mind that they were now living in a new house that they both bought; both partners were on title and on the mortgage even though the husband financed most of it. The wife had initially contacted a mediator, but her husband was ambivalent thinking that if he hired an attorney it might be best for him. His goal was to pay her off the minimum amount of money that would end the marriage.

If the husband chose a litigating route he would hire an attorney, file a petition for dissolution, and encourage his wife to also hire one. Both parties would then be locked in an adversarial dynamic with two attorneys who would try to maximize the return of their respective clients. The husband's $300,000 salary, the $750,000 house, their joint 401K accumulations, and other savings would be tirelessly fought over until one or both of the parties gave in or gave up. In this case, the legal fees would be substantial, especially given that there would be two instead of one, and especially if the case proceeded through the court system. Additionally, family members and acquaintances back home would be reactive about the choice of method of resolution, which would have some negative repercussions for the husband in the future. Even though the wife would get some savings, some 401K, and a short-term spousal maintenance, legal fees would comprise a substantial percentage given that the marriage was only three years in length.

In terms of game theory, in the litigation route, the husband would assume a dominating, aggressive strategy, defecting from the marital covenant, and defecting from a mutually cooperative strategy. He would be looking for the best possible outcome for himself but not for his wife, and his focus was solely on money and the speed with which he could get her out of his life. Unfortunately, as we have seen, this approach to conflict within the PDG eventually arouses the other party's attention, causing them to also "defect" from cooperation—perhaps in increments but slowly moving away from a mutual solution to a litigated solution. She, in return, might play the victim game and stall the process, not yet having accepted her husband's intention. Unfortunately, these anxiety-aggression games increase time, stress, professional fees, and the overall duration of the process. Their Nash Equilibrium is precisely as we would expect, with both parties in a condition of mutual defection, neither one of them willing to start moving toward a cooperative solution—with a large price to pay. Eventually, a court would order short-term spousal support and a transfer of money from the husband to the wife. Because of the zero-sum strategy and the defection from a joint, positive and constructive solution, both parties would end up getting less than they would from a cooperative mediation, as follows.

If the parties hired a mediator this would give the parties control over the outcome of their case and allow them both to move on without additional trauma and stress. The process itself would regulate their tendencies toward aggression and bring them back to the most cooperative solution. The Nash Equilibrium would emerge from a set of trusting cooperative behaviors that would insure the best possible result for each of them and both of them together. If either party defected from this dynamic, they would lose in the long run because it would drive the action toward litigation and loss for both parties. Mediation would increase the value of the marital estate for a number of reasons: the wife might eventually get a job; they could agree that she could live in the marital house for a while; perhaps he'd even arrange for her to live in it and take over payments (which would require help from her parents) and ownership. They would have time to consider tax consequences, their housing needs and preferences, and for her, whether she might return to her home country. With cooperation and less anxiety, the parties could carefully think things through without having to make anxiety-ridden decisions.

Now it is time to discuss the Prisoner's Dilemma based on what we have learned. At the end of this chapter you will see a diagram that exemplifies a new way of approaching the strategic divorce situation that is based on an educational phase before the mediation begins—and during the process. In this new strategic situation, the parties have been made aware of the Prisoner's Dilemma, how it works in divorce, and how they can overcome tendencies toward fear and defection.

Recall that in the original position described in the Prisoner's Dilemma, there are a few assumptions that we should highlight. The situation is uncertain because neither one knows what the other will do. There is a question about trust. In the classic PDG, the parties are thieves, and in principle are involved in harming the interests of others. Thus, it is not unreasonable that both parties would distrust each other. In the classical case, the parties are precluded from speaking to each other so it would be difficult for them to change their level of trust. There are other assumptions perhaps but these three are enough to provide the classic analysis that ends in an unfortunate Nash Equilibrium. We can take this kind of logic and transfer it to the divorce situation as follows.

Most divorcing spouses oscillate between cooperation and competition during the process. From a psychological point of view they deal with anxiety and fear, which causes them to be self-protective, and a higher-order rationality, which includes moral traits like empathy, cooperation, and flexibility. All the reasons that caused the marriage to break down are also present in the divorce mediation, including lack of trust, fear and perception of ongoing harm, and a lack of productive communication. This is exactly why the typical divorce that ends up in litigation is very analogous to the classic Prisoner's Dilemma: fear of ongoing harm, distrust, and unproductive and highly adversarial communication. However, a well-designed mediation process can erode the very assumptions in the following ways.

Even though the marriage broke down for the two parties, a good mediator can facilitate the building of trust in the mediation process. This occurs through the signing of a mediation agreement and engagement letter, an educational phase, a careful outline of the rules and expectations, and a series of interim agreements that build confidence in the process. In turn, these mutual benefit, trust-building agreements overcome perceptions of ongoing harm, and thereby create a new type of communication—one that is non-zero-sum in kind—and this fuels the process toward resolution. Thus, there is a real difference between a typical Prisoner's Dilemma type of dissolution game and a transformed game that overcomes these assumptions. Let's proceed further.

In this new type of strategic decision-making, the parties are made aware of the Prisoner's Dilemma outcomes. They know fully well that if there is an element of distrust both parties could easily choose to defect from full cooperation, thereby ending in the Nash Equilibrium whereby both parties go to prison for six years each. It is important to note this carefully, and not to pass over it too quickly. Because the parties know that thinking in distrustful ways would always result in a defection from full cooperation, thereby leading to mutual defection, they tend away from this orientation. Furthermore, there are ways to gain evidence that the other party is fully cooperating, which demonstrates the value of making and following through on interim, small-risk agreements. It is also true that one of the parties has to make the first cooperative move, which is a very different phenomenon than what we see in a competitive and adversarial dynamic.

Because there is actually a different conflict dynamic in mediation than there is in litigation, it is illegitimate to assess the rationality of a cooperative negotiation from the point of view of an adversarial perspective. The fact of the matter is that when the parties are able to adjust their respective consciousness from competition to cooperation, the Prisoner's Dilemma assumptions dissipate. This allows a radically different kind of game to be played; it is a cooperative and mutual game, one that is constructive and positive for both. By looking at the classical approach to the Prisoner's Dilemma, mediation parties can see how acting "rationally" in this scenario results in poor and harmful consequences for both parties. It is also true that by understanding a transformed Prisoner's Dilemma, one in which the definition of "rationality" is also transmuted, the parties will be eager to make an initial cooperative move. By derivation, the other party's response to an initial cooperation is cooperative as well. This sets a non-zero-sum pattern of behavior that leads to interim agreements, and a final agreement that is the product of mutual cooperation. It involves a more developed rationality, an ability to cope with anxiety, a willingness to communicate cooperatively and productively, and a motivation to build trust. In short, it is smarter and more empathic.

Diagram #3
(Revised/Transformed Prisoner's Dilemma in Divorce w/Education)

Evolved Experience of the Prisoner's Dilemma in Divorce Context post-education phase with qualified mediator creates reflective and cooperative interpretation of the so-called "Dilemma"

Husband

	Cooperates	Competes
Cooperates	decreases fees, duration, stress; makes co-parenting positive	drives process toward litigation
Competes	drives process toward litigation	greatly increases fees, frustration, duration, stress; makes co-parenting difficult

Wife

*decreases stress
*decreases tendency for aggressive games
*increases patience and reflective capacity
*increases creative problem-solving ability
*enhances sympathy and empathy toward conflict partner
*deepens ability to cooperate and to trust
*increases probability to create non-zero-sum outcomes

Chapter 8

Final Thoughts

We are now in the final thoughts of our introduction to game theory and mediation. My hope is that by now any interested reader will have a basic understanding of game theory and its application to mediation. There is much work to be done concerning the application of game theory to cooperative conflict resolution work, and we are already diligently at work to produce the next volume in this series, which will be at an intermediate level. It is, therefore, the right place to leave the reader with a series of problems, questions, and considerations in preparation for this next volume. Let's frame them in terms of what we do know and what we don't know.

We do know that in mediation both parties always play a game of some sort. This is not negative, but instead, is a way that humans deal with the stress and anxiety that comes from uncertainty, along with complex sets of emotions that emerge from a marital uncoupling. We also know that it is normal for individuals to oscillate between feeling cooperative with their conflict partner and protective of their own interests. We can see this oscillation manifest itself in day-to-day and week-to-week behavioral dynamics between the parties. If, for example, a party is feeling confident and safe, she normally will be open to more collaboration and cooperation. If, on the other hand, a party is feeling distrustful or unsafe, then she might tend toward protective and uncooperative. This oscillation can be managed through careful communication within the mediation process.

We also know that the parties may not be fully aware of their needs and preferences, or divided about their needs and preferences without full awareness. A party's level of awareness about these matters can greatly affect a game theory analysis in at least two ways: one, the clarification itself makes the process more accurate and thereby creates more resolutions options; and two, clarification of divisions within one person greatly increases chances that two people can come to mutual benefit agreements and win-win outcomes. We might note at this juncture that conflict itself can often be driven primarily because of a person's lack of clarity or ambivalence: Once these lacunae are cleared up, resolution options usually become readily apparent. We also know, and this is related to the problem concerning a lack of clarity, that most married people who enter mediation have some level of trust and motivation toward cooperation with each other. This is the level of good faith and fair dealing, basic human standards of fairness and justice, and residual feelings of sympathy and care from the marital union. In these cases, much aggression is internally based and, once worked through, dissipates in such a way that true, rational and productive cooperation is possible.

We also know that a game theory approach improves rational thinking. It lays out the options that people have to choose from, and does this in a neutral and unbiased way. By delineating joint choices, the parties can form a detailed, comprehensive view of the conflict situation and its likely outcome paths. Because subjective values and material resources comprise a closed analytic system, the parties can calculate fair and reasonable outcomes that are guided by independent standards. This, in turn, creates — as I have stated — negotiation stabilization and higher resolution potentials. In addition, understanding game theory concepts, including zero-sum games, non-zero-sum games, minimax and maximin, something about the Prisoner's Dilemma, and ways of transforming competition into cooperation, can greatly improve a party's abilities to participate in a positive and constructive process that leads to win-win outcomes. Now let's discuss some of the mysteries that still remain, ones that we will take up in the next volume of this book series.

We do want to know more about the underlying mathematical analysis of the divorce situation in cases of mediation. We want to be able to take a narrative description of a case and convert it into a Prisoner's Dilemma type matrix so that we can not only analyze the situation but also be able to dialogue about it with clients. We want to understand all the tangible factors that go into such a game analysis, including subjective factors and unconscious factors, and factors that are difficult to articulate. We want to understand how personality types affect this process. We want to know more games that parties play, how games change during the mediation, and how we can transform these games into positive and constructive, cooperative strategies that lead to sustainable outcomes. Nevertheless, if we have awakened interest in understanding how game theory contributes to a deeper and broader discussion in mediation theory, then the efforts involved in this book shall have been well conceived.

List of Diagrams in the Text

Some Recommended Reading

The Myth of Mediation Neutrality, Kevin Boileau, EPIS Press, 2014

Mediation: Skills and Techniques, Michael Colatrella, LexisNexis, 2008

Mediation: A Psychological Insight into Conflict Resolution, Freddie Strasser and Paul Randolph, Bloomsbury Academic, 2004.

The Promise of Mediation: The Transformative Approach to Conflict, Robert Baruch A. Bush and Joseph P. Folger, Jossey-Bass, 2004.

The Mediation Process: Practical Strategies for Resolving Conflict, Christopher Moore, Jossey-Bass, 2014.

Mediation Theory and Practice, Suzanne McCorkle and Melanie J. Reese, SAGE, 2014.

Mediation: Practice, Policy, and Ethics, 2nd, Carrie J. Menkel-Meadow, Aspen, 2013.

The Middle Voice: Mediation Conflict Successfully, 2nd, Joseph B. Stulberg and Lela P. Love, Carolina Academic Press, 2013.

The Mediator's Handbook, Revised and Expanded, 4th, Jennifer E. Beer and Caroline C. Packard, New Society Publishers, 2012.

Negotiation: Processes for Problem Solving, Carrie Menkel-Meadow and Anderea K. Schneider, Aspen, 2006.

Getting to Yes, Roger Fisher, William Ury, Bruce Patton, Penguin, 2011.

Game Theory: A Very Short Introduction, Ken Binmore, OUP Oxford, 2007.

Game Theory, Steven Tadelis, Princeton University, 2013.

Index

BCS

This book was written under the auspices and authority of the BCS Dispute Resolution Research Institute of North America. The institute has a number of research projects with the mission to lead to a deeper understanding of conflict and the different strategies humans use for resolution. Some of the major projects involve psychoanalysis, phenomenology, and the mathematics of game theory. The Institute also has an active mediation training program with beginning, intermediate, and advanced courses that are taught on ground and in webinar formats.

www.bcsmediationtraining.com
www.boileaucs.com

For more information on training and mediation write us at:
solutionsbcs@gmail.com

About EPIS Press

We established EPIS Press in the objective of publishing new work in the following areas of inquiry:

1) existential psychoanalysis & phenomenology;

2) traditional & contemporary psychoanalysis theoretical and clinical;

3) critical philosophy as it pertains to psychoanalysis, culture, phenomenology, and philosophy of mind;

4) new literature in phenomenology and psychoanalysis;

5) any related work as it bears on these issues, including neuropsychology and psychoanalysis.

For more information go to
EPIS Press
31 Fort Missoula Road
Suite 4
Missoula, MT 59804
epispublishing1@gmail.com
www.episworldwide.com

CPSIA information can be obtained at www.ICGtesting.com
Printed in the USA
LVOW06s2158100915

453760LV00013B/478/P